For Dana

Best Wishes

Linda

Autism
Living with My Brother Tiger

Jason's story as told by Linda Lee

Illustrated by Penny Lane-Garver

Special Needs Publishing

This book is available at special discounts when purchased in bulk for educational, fund-raising, premium or promotional purposes.

Quotations used by permission from:

AUTISM SPECTRUM DISORDERS by Chantal Sicile-Kira, copyright © 2004 by Chantal Sicile-Kira. Used by permission of Berkley Publishing Group, a division of Penguin Group (USA) Inc.

and

From THE CHILD WITH SPECIAL NEEDS by Dr Stanley Greenspan, copyright © 1998 Used by permission of Perseus Books Group

For details please contact:
Special Needs Publishing, 4742 Liberty Road S, #198, Salem, OR 97302
www.specialneedspublishing.com

Lee, Linda
Autism: Living with my brother Tiger
ISBN Soft Cover 1-59876-007-6
ISBN Hard Cover 1-59876-008-4
1.   Autism - Popular works. 2. Autism in children – Popular works. 3. Title

Printed in China

Cover and book design and production by Patty Arnold, Menagerie Design and Publishing www.menageriedesign.net

Dedication

This book is dedicated to my mother

who taught me that love is not

about saying, it's about doing.

Table of Contents

Autism: Living with My Brother Tiger
Foreword
Margaret L. Bauman, MD

Autism is a behaviorally defined disorder, first described by Dr. Leo Kanner in 1943. Clinical characteristics include impaired social interaction, delayed and disordered language/communication skills, and isolated areas of interest. In addition, some autistic children show repetitive and stereotypic behaviors, have difficulty with transitions, prefer routines, show limited pretend play and have poor eye contact. Autism is believed to be the result of atypical brain development, most probably beginning before birth. Although the cause remains unknown, family studies have provided evidence for a strong genetic liability, but environmental factors may also play a role. Recent epidemiological studies suggest that the prevalence of the Autism Spectrum Disorders (ASD) is now 60 per 10,000 or 1 in 166 children.

A variety of brain abnormalities have been described in autism, including the frequent appearance of increased brain size during early childhood. At the microscopic level, abnormalities have been described in the limbic system, a part of the brain responsible for learning, memory, emotion, and behavior. The cerebellum, located in the back part of the brain, is also abnormal and may be responsible for difficulty with attention, some motor skills and sensory processing, as well as aspects of language, anticipation, and mental imagery. Other areas of the brain, including regions of the cerebral cortex and brainstem, have also been implicated but have been less well studied. In addition to these structural findings, abnormalities have also been found in several neurotransmitters, chemical substances that help nerve cells talk to each other. These neurobiological leads, along with questions pertaining to the role of immune and/or brain growth factors, remain important areas of active research.

Because autism is believed to be a disorder of prenatal onset, there is now an increased effort to identify children at risk as early as possible. A number of clinical research projects are ongoing, looking specifically for clinical "red flags" as early as 4 to 6 months of age. Research suggests that early identification and treatment may result in improved developmental outcomes. However, autism remains a complex disorder with wide clinical variation and best strategies for intervention are not always clear. Approaches that may be effective for one child may not be helpful for another. Clinics and programs that provide a multidisciplinary approach to the diagnosis and management of ASD children remain important resources but many are short staffed and over subscribed. In the future, it will be important to develop additional "medical homes" where these medically and behaviorally challenging children can receive knowledgeable care and where families can find credible information, guidance, and support.

Once a child is diagnosed with autism, parents are all too often left to negotiate their way through the medical and educational world with little guidance. Identifying and forming a team of trusted, experienced professionals is critical to the management of the child over time. As Jason and Tiger's story attests, the good news is that with appropriate services, strong family support, and intensive educational and therapeutic interventions, sizeable numbers of autistic children can and do make significant progress. Parents play a pivotal role in this story. It is they who are the most knowledgeable about their child and, given that knowledge, must collaborate effectively with the medical and educational community. Navigating these uncharted waters can be frightening, difficult, and frequently frustrating but the reward in the end can be without parallel.

Dr. Margaret Bauman

Director of LADDERS, Learning and Developmental Disabilities Evaluation and Rehabilitation Services: Massachusetts General Hospital for Children
Associate Professor of Neurology, Harvard Medical School

Dr. Bauman has devoted much of her medical career to improving the lives of special needs patients, adolescents, and adults, with particular interest in autism. As Director and Founder of the LADDERS program she is a dedicated pediatric neurologist who combines clinical practice with cutting-edge scientific research. Over 20 years ago she co-authored a research paper that identified for the first time anatomic brain abnormalities in autism.

The LADDERS program provides quality diagnostic, treatment, and advocacy for children and their families, with almost 4000 patient visits annually, over 85% having a diagnosis of autism. Physicians including developmental pediatricians, neurologists, gastroenterologists and psychiatrists work collaboratively with occupational, speech and physical therapists, social workers, and educational experts to develop, implement, and support the optimum intervention plan for patients and their families.

Dr. Bauman is also the Medical Director of the ATN, Autism Treatment Network, founded in 2004, a group of doctors, researchers, and parents from around the country working together with the common goal of developing effective medical treatments and evidence-based best practices for individuals with autism.

Jason's Story

My name is Jason. I am 8 years old. I live in America.

My Daddy is Korean and my Mommy is from Ireland. That makes me Eurasian. I have my Daddy's dark hair and eyes and don't look a bit like my Mommy.

This is the story of my family and how everything changed when my brother was born.

When there was just the three of us, my Mommy, my Daddy and me, we used to travel together to foreign countries to do volunteer work. My Daddy is an orthopedic surgeon and sometimes he would be the only one in the whole country.

In Bhutan the airport had dirt floors and Mommy tells me that I used to drag my blanket along the floor kicking up dust. I was not even two then so it was OK to carry my blanket.

These countries did not even have fridges in the homes or shops.

If you bought a chicken at the market, it would come with all the fluffy white feathers, bright yellow beak, and a big long neck with a head. It was dead.

My Mommy would pluck off all the feathers and clean out the inside. My Daddy did not even like to look at it, but he would eat it when it was cooked.

Back then we all used to have a lot of fun. Mommy and
　　　Daddy liked to dance and they would practice in the
　　　kitchen. I would dart between them when they were
　　　doing their spins. Sometimes we would all collide,
　　　or I would get squished.

Daddy even had a cowboy hat and boots. Mommy would
　　　always tell him he looked very cute with his hat on.

Then when I was 3 ½ it all changed.

My Mommy and Daddy had a new baby. They were very
    happy and excited. They said they wanted someone
    for me to play with, but something was wrong.
    He screamed almost all the time.

New babies are supposed to sleep a lot, at least that is what
I was told, but this one didn't. He didn't sleep much
day or night and he *growled*.

We nicknamed him Tiger, but his real name is Christian.
I don't think he knows that because we still call
him Tiger.

At my preschool my teachers were excited too and used to ask me about our new baby. I was not excited, and for weeks only answered one thing, "I do not want to talk about that baby."

They thought that was funny. I did not.

After my brother was born, my Daddy seemed to work a lot more and when he was home he was quiet.

My Mommy and I used to do puzzles and sit together and watch my favorite shows, but she was tired and quiet, too. Sometimes I would notice my Mommy crying but she always said she was OK.

My brother screamed a lot and I would put my hands over my ears. That hardly helped. I called it his **sonic scream**. I would go into the other room to play my Nintendo or Game Boy, but even then with the door shut I could hear his screaming.

When he was little my Mommy said he was screaming because of colic; later she thought it might be his teeth. I didn't know because even after he had all his teeth, he screamed just as much and still didn't sleep.

When we tried to go anywhere in the car, Tiger would
   scream fiercely the whole time. He would cry so hard
   that the tears would shoot out of his eyes and not even
   touch his cheeks. Sometimes he would throw up.
   Ughhhh. That made me feel like throwing up, too.

We stopped going places and I had to give up my
   Tae Kwon Do.

We used to have friends and new people over for dinner often, but Tiger did not like other people. He would rush to the front door and shove on their legs to get them back out the door, then slam it in their face. We stopped having people over for dinner.

On my brother's second birthday he did not like the cake, or the "Happy Birthday" song and the candles terrified him. He hated the presents and did not know that there were toys inside the wrapping paper.

At that time he did not play with toys anyway; instead he always carried around a little branch that all the grapes had been taken off. He would spend hours every day spinning it close to his eyes. He even took it to bed with him and in the morning he would still be holding it tightly. Eventually it would get moldy and smelly.

When my brother was just over two they told us he had *autism*. My Mommy and Daddy were very sad. I didn't know what autism meant and they said neither did they.

My Mommy took away Tiger's milk because a neighbor told her that might help. My Daddy thought it sounded a little crazy. Tiger started to get better and to do the same things I was doing, like jumping off the couch. He even screamed less and started to sleep more. He looked at us for the first time and waved "Good-bye."

Even though my brother started to get slowly better he was still very difficult to live with. Sometimes my brother did funny things, like the time he walked on the ironing board. It made a funny squeaky noise.

He did not fall off and the ironing board did not topple over, but it surprised Mommy.

Other times he did dangerous things like crawling across the stove when Mommy had pots cooking. She said she had to watch him every second and couldn't even turn her back on him.

Mommy mostly stopped cooking. I don't think she likes to cook anyway; she would rather sew. Sometimes she lets me sew on her machine, too.

Tiger used to climb on the Outside of the stairs and
hang off the balcony. He would run on top of the
camper, too. It was very scary.

We moved to a house with no stairs and a big backyard.
Mommy and Daddy spent a whole summer building a
tall fence. They shouldn't have bothered because Tiger
would not go out in the backyard at that house. That
made my parents very sad.

Tiger used to run away a lot. He loved to bolt down the middle of double yellow lines and he would laugh like crazy. One time after church he ran straight out into the middle of the busy road and my Mommy ran right after him. She didn't even look to see if a car was coming. That was very scary for me and my Mommy said my face was as white as a ghost.

Daddy put bolts at the top of all our doors so that Tiger couldn't escape anymore.

When we would try to eat dinner, it was very noisy. Tiger used to drag at Mommy or Daddy to try and get them away from the table. If they would not leave, he would climb on their heads like a cat.

My Daddy likes to be left alone while he eats. Mommy says Daddy is like a dog with a bone.

For years my brother had trouble wearing clothes and shoes.
It was like everything was hurting him. My Mommy
would buy him shoes and she would run back and
forward over them with the wheel of the minivan to try
and soften them up. He still would not wear them and
of course they were so beaten up she could not take
them back to the store. For years he wore no socks
or shoes, even in the rain and snow.

Sometimes I used to feel very embarrassed about how Tiger looked. He would wear the same clothes every day and sleep in them at night for weeks at a time without being changed. Often they were all stained and ripped with the knees hanging out of his pants.

Mommy would try to change him but it was impossible. At church he would look very funny among all these dressed-up people, but Mommy said it was not important how he looked on the outside, because God looks at our *hearts*.

For some reason Tiger could not bear to be touched. Daddy would strap him in the high chair and Mommy would hold Tiger as they tried to cut his hair but he would go completely frantic and couldn't bear if even a tiny hair landed on his cheek. He looked like he was trying to get out of his skin.

Mommy started to cut his hair in bed while he was fast asleep in the dark. Sometimes he would wake up in the middle and then he would look really funny the next day with half a haircut.

Every time we tried to bathe Tiger it was a big, big fight.
Mommy would get very upset because Tiger would not
let her take off his clothes and he would struggle and
struggle. He would scream so loud, especially in the
water, like it was hurting him.

Then one day Mommy said, "That's it, I'm never bathing
him again." Daddy was a little surprised, but she
said that if we lived in Africa it wouldn't matter.
So he didn't have a bath for over a year.

Then one day while Mommy was in the bath, he took off his clothes and just climbed in beside her. She had not even asked him to get in. Now he often takes a bath and he stays in for a long time playing with toys and bubbles.

Mommy puts Epsom Salts in our bath and they feel like crunchy pebbles under my feet until they dissolve. It is supposed to help get rid of bad stuff from our bodies.

My parents used to think that Tiger would never speak. He was almost three before he even said "Mom."

When we were trying to teach Tiger to talk, my Mommy and I used to play a game with him in the car. I would start to sing and this always made Tiger scream, then Mommy would say, "Use your words, Tiger, say 'Stop'." Then we made him say, "Stop, Jason." Eventually he could say "Stop singing, Jason." It took him weeks to get that far. I don't think Tiger knew it was a game, because sometimes he would start screaming and would scream the whole way home.

Tiger got better and better and on his third birthday my parents were very weird. They were looking into his diaper and Mommy was crying because Tiger had his first almost normal poop. Before that he always had stinking, watery poop that would run down his legs and onto his feet.

I would leave the room when they changed him because it smelled so bad and Tiger's bum would be all burned and sore and he would scream like crazy. It would happen lots of times during the day.

I help my Mommy and Daddy take care of Tiger. If he gets
    food he shouldn't eat, like gluten or sugar, he goes out
    of control. It is not just foods, some smells like gas
    fumes or dry erasable markers make him crazy, too.
    He screams, bangs his head on the floor, and gets
    awful diarrhea again. He doesn't sleep either.

Every Sunday we go to the Vietnamese restaurant after
    church to eat rice noodles. My important job is to
    crawl around the floor and make sure there is no
    candy on the floor. If Tiger gets it he will eat it
    and then be sick for days.

Because of Tiger we cannot all do things together anymore. I get to do **special** things with my Daddy like watch movies, eat ice cream and go to Korea.

My Mommy takes me out on Friday's, to eat chocolate cake. I get the "Barney's Blackout" cake and my Mom just gets a pot of tea. She always asks for a few bites of my cake though.

When I was only seven I got to fly to California all alone to see my grandma, Halmoni. At the airport they put a big tag around my neck that I was not allowed to take off. I had a secret password that only my Mommy and Grandma knew.

At first I was scared but my parents told me that I could be a brave boy and I was. I was glad I went because I had a lot of fun and got to go to Disneyland and Legoland with my cousins.

I go to Catholic school even though I am not Catholic.
Every morning in prayers I pray for Tiger. My Mommy
did not know that but my teacher told her at teacher
conference. That made my Mommy cry. My teacher
tells me that I am very smart and kind. I got an
award for being a *peacemaker*.

One day last year an older boy was trying to bully me.
I told my parents and they asked me what did I do.
I answered, "I didn't say or do anything, but I thought
to myself that he shouldn't mess with a second grader
who knew long division."

They laughed.

I like to do **puzzles** or play Nintendo but Tiger will often not leave me alone. He wrecks my puzzles and will not let me play Monopoly. Sometimes that makes me very angry and I take my pillow and lock myself in the bathroom so that I can get peace to do what I like to do. I lie on the floor and read Calvin and Hobbes.

My Mommy tells me that having Tiger as a brother has made me very patient. If he acts weird while we are out I just tell people that my brother is autistic and he cannot help it.

Sometimes I have friends over, but not very often. We try to play computer games or Nintendo but it is very difficult. Tiger will only let us play games he wants to play and he screams if we don't. I don't think my friends understand. I like to go to their houses because then we can play whatever we like and don't have to think about Tiger or listen to his screaming.

My Mommy and Daddy have a website and I got to record my voice for the stories about getting blood drawn. If you click on www.helpautismnow.com you can hear my voice. My brother likes to look at the storybooks and he knows the stories by heart. Sometimes even when we are in the car he will say them.

Now that Tiger is five and has improved so much he is much easier to live with. Some days he doesn't even scream once. He has lots of words; his favorites right now are "No," "Not yet," and "Later."

He likes to chase me on his tricycle all around the house, he only just learned how to ride that and Mommy told me I knew how when I was only eighteen months old. He is far too big for the tricycle.

Tiger goes to a special school. He gets to ride the yellow bus. He can spell his name and count to 60. He knows which video he wants to watch by the writing on the label. When he was younger he used to line up the video covers all the way along the floor and into the dining room.

He used to line up everything, even the food he was going to eat. Now he doesn't line up stuff anymore.

He can even go potty at times, at least for number 1.

A few weeks ago we had a lot of snow here in Oregon.
Daddy wanted to go sledding but Mommy said,
"No Way" because the last time we took Tiger it
was so awful. He would not wear a coat or shoes
and socks and he hated the cold and the snow.

This time he wore boots, mittens, a jacket, and a furry
headband. He grabbed the sled and jumped in it all
by himself, going "Wheeeeeeeeeeeeeeeee" down
the hill. Then he dragged the sled back up the hill and
went down over and over again. My parents said they
wished they had brought the camera but even when
they do bring it they always forget to take pictures.

Tiger used to hate us to hug or kiss him. He would scream and rub our kisses off furiously; sometimes he even punched Mommy in the face. He would never sit on Mommy's knee.

Now he is very loving and kind. He gives us kisses often and even asks for them. He likes to sit on Mommy's knee. One day out of the blue he was sitting on her lap and he looked into her eyes and said, "I love you." Of course she cried, but this time it was a happy cry.

Sometimes my parents puzzle me. Recently they were very excited because Tiger had told his first lie. They invited friends over and opened a bottle of champagne. I got to clink my water glass with them, too.

They puzzle me because when I told a lie a long time ago they certainly did not celebrate. I got a big *serious* lecture.

My Mom and Dad tell me that I am very, very unique because God chose me **specially** to have a brother with autism.

I believe them.

I don't think that any of my friends would have patience for Tiger. I suppose God knew that, too.

Final Thoughts from Tiger's Mom

As you can probably imagine by reading between the lines, living with Tiger has not always been exactly easy (from a Mom's perspective). In fact, there was a time when Tiger was around two, when my husband and I decided that if he never spoke, and never was potty trained, it would be OK, just so long as he would stop SCREAMING!!!

Well, as you can tell from Jason's story, Tiger has come a long way from then. Nowadays, we look back on that time and cringe, grateful that we have all survived. This story, never mind this book, would not have been possible without the support of so many people in our lives. We have been blessed with dozens of dedicated professionals who have worked directly and indirectly with Tiger over the years, including autism specialists, teachers, teacher's assistants, speech and occupational therapists, physicians, and caregivers. Their compassion and commitment to Tiger and our family has been truly inspiring, and I am deeply grateful to them all.

Even though I had spent over 20 years in nursing, and most of that as an RN in emergency rooms, I knew absolutely nothing about autism when Tiger was first diagnosed. It was just not part of our training, and at that time I considered it to be a rare, hopeless, and untreatable, psychiatric condition.

After his diagnosis, just after he turned two, I was so sleep deprived and SO desperate that I was willing to try anything, even something as crazy as taking away his milk. Back then, for me, the idea of "treating" the psychiatric condition of autism with special diets seemed totally absurd. Yet, the more I read, the more I discovered that some children with autism may have underlying biological issues.* These may include gut problems, like gastritis and colitis, diminished enzymes that break down foods, antioxidant enzyme deficiencies, low sulfate, and detoxification issues. It is these abnormalities that special diets attempt to address.

One by one, I started looking at all the things in Tiger's environment that might have been affecting him negatively, and to my surprise there were many. After a few months *(*see Studies page 48)*

of making these changes he had lost all his self-injurious behaviors and started to sleep all night. For a sleep deprived, "ready to go mad" mother it was little short of miraculous. Some things that we tried worked, and some didn't. I think that THAT is the key to remember. Certain things work well for one child but have absolutely no effect on another. Children with autism are all uniquely different.

Each child affected may have the general label of autism, but what exactly does that mean? Saying a child has autism is the equivalent of looking out the window and thinking, well, that's a bird. A bird is a bird, and they all have feathers and fly. But there are thousands of assorted birds, and they are all different. A penguin and a robin have very little in common. Although almost all birds fly, they do so in different ways. Some soar gracefully on the air currents and others flap furiously (no pun intended).

Similarly with our kids with autism, they may have feathers and fly, i.e., have social and communication issues, but any "treatment" geared at autism in general may have limited or no value for a specific child. It is a little like clothing that claims to be one-size-fits-all. That may be true, but it may also mean that it fits no one particularly well.

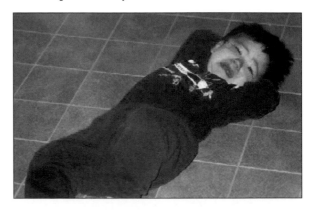

I like the way Dr. Stanley Greenspan talks about this issue in his book, *The Child with Special Needs*:

"Many children today are given labels that are misleading. Instead of pinpointing a child's unique strengths and challenges, they obscure them and unwittingly demoralize and create negative expectations on the part of parents, therapists and teachers."

I think parents, working collaboratively with the professionals, are in the perfect position to develop an individualized plan that is best suited for their child's exact needs, as determined by the child's strengths and weaknesses.

To go back to the birds, it would be a waste of time to teach a robin how to live in the Antarctic, and a penguin would likely not benefit from flying lessons.

As parents we may be tempted to leave it all up to the professionals, but no one can possibly know our child the way we as parents do. The professionals need our information to decide on the best course of action. With that in mind, I encourage parents to become experts in **their own** child. Read, ask questions, and study the Internet. But beware—a recent search for autism treatments turned up 1,333,000 options, and few, if any, of these have been "scientifically proven." I like how Chantal Sicile-Kira puts it in her excellent book, *Autism Spectrum Disorders: The Complete Guide to Understanding Autism*:

"I liken getting information from the Internet to talking to strangers in a bar. You never know who you are talking to until you investigate and ask a few questions."

I personally found that other parents who had successfully implemented interventions I was contemplating were excellent sources of information.

Start slowly and do one thing at a time. Be content with tiny changes and try not to compare your child to another of the same chronological age, since few things can cause your heart to sink more rapidly. For example, in Tiger's case, at two and a half years of age he had a developmental age of three months in certain areas. I was devastated when I compared him to a child of the same age, or even a younger typical child. But, comparing him to a three-month-old, I would not have expected him to start speaking immediately, no matter what I did.

Most importantly, choose something and start TODAY. Lastly, refuse to quit! Remember, action is empowering, regardless of the outcome.

Today, Tiger is attending a first grade Life Skills program, and his teachers not only say he is doing great but also they genuinely seem to enjoy him. He takes field trips on regular buses, and goes to the library and grocery stores. He has hundreds of words and speaks in full sentences. He plays Nintendo with his brother and doesn't mind too much that our house is often full of people again. He takes swimming lessons and can swim unassisted across the pool. Recently we have been able to take him to the zoo, aquarium, and the State Fair.

Most importantly, today I feel incredibly grateful and truly blessed, for all that we have learned and continue to learn about love and life since Tiger came into our lives. He has been for me, truly the greatest inspiration, motivator, and teacher.

References

Studies

Horvath K, Patadimitriou J C, John C, et al. "Gastrointestinal abnormalities in children with autistic disorder." *Journal of Pediatrics*, 1999 Nov: 135(5): 559–563.

Buie T, Pediatric Gastroenterologist, Harvard, Massachusetts General Hospital, MA. "Gastrointestinal function of children with autism" *Initial Autism Research Findings*.

Knivsberg A M, Reichelt K L, Hoien T, Nodland M. "A randomized, controlled study of dietary intervention in autistic syndromes." *Nutritional Neuroscience*, 2002 Vol 5(4), 251–261.

Waring R H, Klovrza L V. "Sulphur metabolism in autism." *Journal of Nutritional and Environmental Medicine* (2000)10, 25–32.

Alberti A, Pirrone P, Elia M, Waring R H, Romano C. "Sulphation deficit in "low-functioning" autistic children: a pilot study." *Biological Psychiatry* 1999:46; 420–424.

Yorbik O, Sayal A, Akay C, et al. "Investigation of antioxidant enzymes in children with autistic disorder." *Prostaglandins Leukot Essent Fatty Acids.* 2002 Nov; 67(5): 341–3.

James S J, Cutler P, Melnyk S, et al. "Metabolic biomarkers of increased oxidative stress and impaired methylation capacity in children with autism." *American Journal of Clinical Nutrition* 2004 Dec: 80(6): 1611–7.

Books

The Child with Special Needs: Encouraging Intellectual and Emotional Growth. Copyright © 1998 by Stanley Greenspan, MD.

www.floortime.org

"Based on two decades of practice and original research into developmental disabilities this essential work helps parents and professionals "get beyond the label" and understand each child's unique profile."

Autism Spectrum Disorders: The Complete Guide to Understanding Autism, Asperger's Syndrome, PDD, and other ASD, by Chantal Sicile-Kira

www.chantalsicile-kira.com

"2005 Autism Society of America Outstanding Literary Work of the Year Award Recipient. The book covers all aspects of autism spectrum disorders from birth to adulthood. The factual information is illustrated by quotes from people on the spectrum, the author's personal experience and opinions from professionals. This user-friendly book includes many practical tips and resources, and is geared towards the general readership, parents, professionals, and anyone who knows someone with an ASD." Extensive website resources included.

Websites
Parents May Find Helpful

ARC of the United States
www.thearc.org

The Arc is the national organization of and for people with mental retardation and related developmental disabilities and their families. It is devoted to promoting and improving supports and services for people with mental retardation and their families. The ARC offers state-specific resource guides. Local chapters nationwide may have availability for respite, sibling workshops and training for parents/caregivers.

Autism Research Unit
http://osiris.sunderland.ac.uk/autism/aru.htm

The Autism Research Unit (ARU) was started in 1982 and is based at the University of Sunderland, England. The two main aims are firstly to provide a basis for research into the possible causes of autism and secondly to provide an accessible store of traditional and current research information on autism. The Unit produces a booklet which gives a full rundown of their current research and a helpful guide for parents/clinicians who are thinking of implementing a gluten-and/or casein-free diet.

Autism Treatment Network

www.autismtreatmentnetwork.org

The Autism Treatment Network is composed of distinguished physicians and researchers from leading medical centers across the country who have joined with other autism experts and parents with the mission to:

1. Provide optimal diagnosis and comprehensive care for individuals with autism through evidence-based practices with specific attention to associated medical conditions.

2. Disseminate this information to healthcare providers, educators, and parents.

3. Promote research aimed at improving treatment for autism.

Autism Research Center
Cambridge University, England

www.autismresearchcenter.com

"The mission of the ARC is to understand the biomedical causes of autism spectrum conditions, and develop new and validated methods for assessment and intervention. The ARC fosters collaboration between scientists in Cambridge University and outside, to accelerate this mission." Co-Director, Dr. Simon Baron-Cohen is the developer of the CHAT screening tool and author of numerous books and research papers.

Autism Research Institute

www.autismresearchinstitute.com

Nonprofit organization established in 1967 by Dr. Bernard Rimland. ARI is primarily devoted to conducting research, and to disseminating the results of research, on the causes of autism and on methods of preventing, diagnosing, and treating autism and other severe behavioral disorders of childhood. Site includes a database covering over two decades of responses from over 21,000 parents on the behavioral effects of biological interventions.

Autism Society of America

www.autism-society.org

"Improving the lives of all affected by autism. Autism Society of America (ASA) is the leading voice and resource of the entire autism community in education, advocacy, services, research, and support. ASA, a chapter-and member-based organization, is committed to meaningful participation and self-determination in all aspects of life for individuals on the autism spectrum and their families. ASA accomplishes its ongoing mission through close collaboration with a successful network of chapters, members, supporters, and organizations."

Autism Speaks

www.autismspeaks.org

Founded in February 2005 by Suzanne and Bob Wright, "Goals are guided by an uncompromising passion to understand this complex disorder and hasten the discovery of a cure. We are committed to raising public awareness about autism and its effects on individuals, families, and society, and to giving hope to all who deal with the hardships of this disorder. We also seek to raise funds to facilitate effective treatment and research on autism. We are dedicated to uncovering the biology of autism and developing effective biomedical treatments through research funding."

Autism Today

www.autismtoday.com

"The website is a creative, interactive, one-stop shop where you can find everything you need to navigate the maze of ASD-related information. With over 2,500 pages of content, it is the largest autism resource online and one of the leading autism and Aspergers resource distributors in the world, and receives over 2 million hits a month. Bookstore, conference listings, online access to experts, etc."

Center for the Study of Autism

www.autism.org

Directed by Dr. Stephen Edelson, the site provides valuable information for parents and professionals on all aspects of autism. Includes information on varying therapies, educational and biological interventions. Provides numerous website links.

Cure Autism Now Foundation (CAN)
www.cureautismnow.org

"An organization of parents, clinicians, and leading scientists committed to accelerating the pace of biomedical research in autism through raising money for research projects, education, and outreach. The organization's primary focus is to fund essential research through a variety of programs designed to encourage innovative approaches toward identifying the causes, prevention, treatment, and a cure for autism and related disorders."

Dan Marino Foundation
www.danmarinofoundation.com

Founded in 1992 by Claire and Dan Marino, a nonprofit organization, supporting programs which provide integrated intervention services for children with special needs—medical, emotional and/or behavioral.

Dan Marino Childnett
www.childnett.tv

A first-of-its-kind Internet web channel dedicated to autism and other neurological disorders.

First Signs
www.firstsigns.org

Resource for parents and professionals regarding normal/typical developmental milestones. May be useful baseline information for parents to discuss with their physician if they have developmental concerns about their child.

Future Horizons
www.futurehorizons-autism.com

Extensive resource for publishing and books relating to the autism spectrum; books and tapes available online. Conferences offered throughout the country featuring autism experts.

Help Autism Now Society (HANS)
www.helpautismnow.com

Creates hands-on, user-friendly tools, primarily geared towards physicians and other professionals, but parents may find the information helpful: over 70 illustrations depicting the "behavioral symptoms" of autism. Online social stories: "Going to See the Doctor" and "Going to Have Blood Drawn" may be helpful in preparing a child with autism for these scenarios. Founded in December 2002 by Paul and Linda Lee, Tiger and Jason's parents.

LADDERS
www.massgeneral.org/mghfc/MGHfC_medspec_ladders_staff.htm

LADDERS, Learning and Developmental Disabilities Evaluation and Rehabilitation Services. Massachusetts General Hospital for Children, Boston, MA.

Dr. Margaret Bauman, who wrote the Foreword for this book, is the Director of this program.

National Alliance for Autism Research (NAAR)
www.naar.org

Established in 1994 by parents of children with autism, NAAR is the first organization in the U.S. dedicated to funding and accelerating biomedical research focusing on autism spectrum disorders. Merged with Autism Speaks in 2005.

National Autistic Society, UK based
http://www.nas.org.uk/

The National Autistic Society exists to champion the rights and interests of all people with autism and to ensure that they and their families receive quality services appropriate to their needs. The website includes information about autism and Asperger syndrome, the NAS and its services and activities. The Society also offers telephone hotline and free parent-to-parent telephone service. Site contains useful information for U.S. citizens as well.

Northwest Autism Foundation
www.autismnwaf.org

"The Northwest Autism Foundation is a nonprofit that provides information and education for professionals, organizations, and families who care for persons with an Autism Spectrum Disorder. The foundation seeks to fulfill this mission by cooperating with organizations and groups involved with any aspect of autism. The foundation publishes a useful Resource Directory listing with particular emphasis on NW resources."

Pubmed
www.ncbi.nim.nih.gov/pubmed

Free, immediate, Internet access to the most up-to-date and previously published medical studies from numerous U.S. and international medical journals. Can be accessed by subject, author, or title of study. Abstracts are often available.

The Schafer Autism Report
www.home.sprynet.com/~schafer

Free, online, daily newsletter that monitors all the major news sources, websites, and the latest research for important and practical news development regarding autism. Studies often available for viewing in advance of publication.

Check out your local newspaper for listings of support groups.

Magazines

Autism Asperger's Digest
www.futurehorizons-autism.com

"Featuring original articles and material from sources around the world, covers the latest people, products, research, news, and viewpoints emerging in the autism field. Full-length excerpts from ground-breaking new books on autism, original articles from top specialists, etc."

The Autism Perspective (TAP)
www.theautismperspective.org

"Provides balanced information on the myriad of therapies and treatments for the vast and complicated realm of ASD without taking sides."

Autism Spectrum Quarterly
www.ASQuarterly.com

"ASQ is described as "the magajournal" to underscore that it combines the readability and interest of a high-level magazine with the substance and depth of a professional journal. Each issue features a line of research and commentary aimed at helping parents, teachers, and clinicians to translate this research into practice."

Spectrum
www.spectrumpublications.com

For parents of children with autism and developmental disabilities. Wide variety of topics covered, including educational, biomedical and research. Contains ASD-specific news articles and interviews with autism experts and mainstream celebrities affiliated with autism.

For Parents Considering Dietary Manipulations

Special Diets for Special Kids by Lisa Lewis PhD

www.autismndi.com

This book not only provides special gluten/casein–free recipes that may be useful for some children with autism, but also has an extensive discussion regarding the scientific studies supporting dietary interventions.

Breaking the Vicious Cycle by Elaine Gottschall

www.pecanbread.com

Focuses on the Specific Carbohydrate diet and the rationale for its use in some children with autism. Recipes and websites also included.

www.gfcfdiet.com

Confers with manufacturers and provides listings of permissible foods on a gluten/casein–free diet. Lists are updated on a regular basis. Pre-packaged gf/cf foods and cooking mixes are readily available. Online support group available.

www.feingold.org

Extensive information regarding salicylates, synthetic food colorings, and additives, etc. Some children with autism may benefit from the elimination of these substances from their diet. Rationale and studies to support these interventions available.

Talk with the folks at your local health store, who often have community notice boards.

The inclusion of websites is for informational purposes only and does not indicate an endorsement of their contents.

Profits from the sale of this book go to support:

Help Autism Now Society

Registered 501c3 nonprofit
www.helpautismnow.com

Penny Lane-Garver, Artist

Penny Lane-Garver has worked in the Early Childhood Education field for over 10 years. Penny believes that some of the most challenging experiences with children have left the deepest impression in her heart, and have taught her more than she could ever have imagined.

Penny has been expressing herself through her art since she was a young child and this book combines both her love of children and art. Penny lives in Salem, Oregon, with her husband, Perry, and daughter, Madeline. She is currently working on her next book. PennyLane817@msn.com

Linda Lee, Author:

Linda Lee moved to the U.S. when she was 27 and has over 20 years of nursing experience, initially in Belfast, Northern Ireland. She has managed Emergency Rooms in Manhattan and Boston.

Linda now lives in Salem, Oregon with her husband, a practicing orthopedic surgeon, and their two sons. After their two-year-old son was diagnosed with autism, they realized that despite all their medical training they knew very little about autism. As a result they founded the nonprofit Help Autism Now Society (HANS) with the goal of helping children and families, by supporting the medical and educational professionals in better understanding of autism.

Linda is the Executive Director of HANS. She is active in giving presentations to medical and educational professionals as well as parents, and developing materials related to autism.

About This Book

This book came about because of a chance comment by Penny, "Have you ever thought of writing a book through Jason's eyes? If you do I would like to illustrate it." She was as good as her word, volunteering her time and talent.

Initially when I asked Jason if he would be interested in helping me write about living with Tiger, he answered immediately, "It's tough. The End." When I told Jason that it would help other kids he answered, "Of course."

Jason is an enormous gift in our lives and wise for his years. He likes to remind Paul and me not to think about the should-haves and could-haves. With autism in the family there are always should-haves and could-haves.

Tiger's artwork at age 6

Testimonials from experts regarding
Autism: Living with My Brother Tiger

"This is a moving, honest, and wonderfully written portrayal of life with autism as seen through the eyes of a sibling. A brilliant introduction to autism for children, it describes how the whole family is affected, yet also includes a great resource section for the adult reader. If you only read one sibling or children's book on autism, this should be it."

Chantal Sicile-Kira

The Complete Guide to Understanding Autism, Asperger's Syndrome, PDD, and other ASD

2005 Autism Society of America Outstanding Literary Work of the Year Award Recipient

"I loved this book—it is such a credit to the wisdom of children! I shared it with my family and they finally understood why I have been so passionate about working with autistic children and their families for over twenty-five years."

Mary Lynn Obrien, MD

Pediatric Developmental Specialist, Kaiser Permanente and Oregon Health Services University (OHSU), Portland, Oregon

"Jason's story provides a voice for siblings of individuals with autism and a bridge to understanding for teachers and friends who seek to support families."

Michelle Pardew, PhD

Professor, Special Education Western Oregon University

"This book is a powerful story of a family's ultimate and unconditional love. The world that Tiger and his family live in is one filled with many challenges laced with constant love. This story is proof that love conquers all. The dedication of Tiger's parents and brother is unsurpassed. Jason often tells his classmates that living with Tiger is his "life-long lesson." *Autism: Living with My Brother Tiger* is a true story of survival and overcoming hardships—a story we all can learn from."

Mari Pat Brooks

Principal—St Joseph's Elementary School Salem, Oregon

"On a daily basis we deal with the effects of autism on our students, their peers, teachers, and classroom staff, and most importantly, their families. Jason's book provides important insights from a sibling's perspective, which would be beneficial for all of us professionals to be aware of when working with children with autism and their families."

Mary Lintz, Occupational Therapist

Salem/Keizer Schools Salem, Oregon

"This book is a poignant, inspirational story of a family's struggles with autism. Written from the perspective of the eight-year-old brother, I found it incredibly moving. Beautifully illustrated, this story is honest, and yet hopeful. I highly recommend it."

Pastor Don Brandt

Our Saviors Lutheran Church Salem, Oregon

Order Books

Help your family member, teacher, physician, or church leader better understand autism by giving them the gift of this book. Check with your local bookstore or order below.

☐ YES, I would like ___ copies of the softcover book at US$15.95 each* plus $4.50 shipping for first book and $2 for each additional book.

☐ YES, I would like ___ copies of the hardcover book at US$19.95 each plus $4.50 shipping for first book and $2 for each additional book.

International shipping, add $9.50 for first book and $5 for each additional book.

International order forms should be accompanied by a postal money order in U.S. funds to cover book and shipping. Please allow 15 days for delivery from receipt of order.

Or order online using Paypal at www.specialneedspublishing.com

Name: _____

Address: _____

City: _____ State: _____ Zip: _____

Telephone: _____

Email address: _____

Please make your check or money order payable and return to:

Special Needs Publishing, 4742 Liberty Road S, #198, Salem OR 97302

Speaking/Seminars: Linda Lee, RN, has been described as having the rare ability to make an audience laugh and cry at the same time. She is active in giving presentations to medical and educational professionals, parents and civic groups, with particular emphasis on the impact that autism has not only on the affected child but also on the family and community. She is available for limited speaking/seminar engagements.

For more information, contact Linda Lee at www.helpautismnow.com

* Special discounts when purchased in bulk for educational, fundraising, premium or promotional purposes.